THE SENSES

Your Senses

CHELSEA
CLUBHOUSE
An Imprint of Chelsea House Publishers
A Haights Cross Communications Company
Philadelphia

Kimberley Jane Pryor

For Nick, Ashley and Thomas

This edition first published in 2004 in the United States of America by Chelsea Clubhouse, a division of Chelsea House Publishers and a subsidiary of Haights Cross Communications.

Chelsea Clubhouse
1974 Sproul Road, Suite 400
Broomall, PA 19008-0914

The Chelsea House world wide web address is www.chelseahouse.com

Library of Congress Cataloging-in-Publication Data

Pryor, Kimberley Jane.
    Your senses / Kimberley Jane Pryor.
    p. cm. — (The senses)

    Includes index.
    Contents: Your senses — Seeing — Hearing — Smelling — Tasting — Touching — Hunger — Thirst — Balance — Pain — Using all your senses.

    ISBN 0-7910-7559-1
    1. Senses and sensation—Juvenile literature. [1. Senses and sensation.] I. Title. II. Series.
    QP434.P79 2004
    612.8—dc21

                                                                                    2003001178

First published in 2003 by
MACMILLAN EDUCATION AUSTRALIA PTY LTD
627 Chapel Street, South Yarra, Australia, 3141

Associated companies and representatives throughout the world.

Copyright © Kimberley Jane Pryor 2003

Page layout by Raul Diche
Illustrations by Alan Laver, Shelly Communications
Photo research by Legend Images

Printed in China

Acknowledgements
Cover photograph: children at birthday celebration, courtesy of Photodisc.

Coo-ee Picture Library, p. 20; The DW Stock Picture Library, pp. 18, 21, 29; Eyewire, p. 28; Getty Images/Image Bank, pp. 8, 25, 26; Getty Images/Stone, pp. 9, 13; Getty Images/Taxi, p. 16; Great Southern Stock, pp. 4, 24, 27; Imageaddict, p. 23; Nick Milton, pp. 6, 10, 14; Photodisc, pp. 1, 5; PhotoEssentials, p. 17; Photolibrary.com/Index Stock, p. 12.

While every care has been taken to trace and acknowledge copyright, the publisher tenders their apologies for any accidental infringement where copyright has proved untraceable. Where the attempt has been unsuccessful, the publisher welcomes information that would redress the situation.

Please note
At the time of printing, the Internet addresses appearing in this book were correct. Owing to the dynamic nature of the Internet, however, we cannot guarantee that all these addresses will remain correct.

Contents

Your Senses

You have five main senses to help you learn about the world. They are sight, hearing, smell, taste, and touch.

Your five main senses tell you about your surroundings.

Your sense of balance helps you to stand on a balance beam.

You also have senses to help you learn about your body and its needs. Some of these senses are hunger, thirst, balance, and pain.

Seeing

You see with your eyes. Light enters the eye through the **cornea**. It passes through the **pupil**. The pupil is the black opening in the colored part of the eye called the iris. The pupil changes size. In dim light, it grows larger to let more light into the eye. In bright light, the pupil becomes smaller.

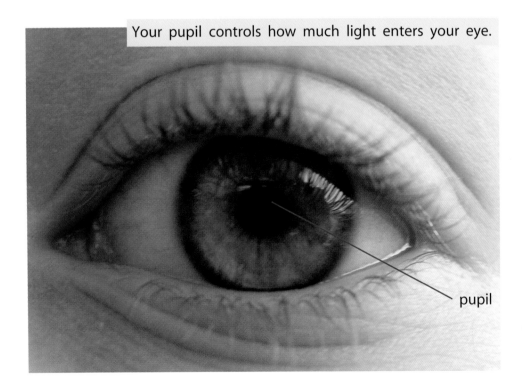

Your pupil controls how much light enters your eye.

pupil

Inside the eye, light passes through the **lens**. The lens **focuses** the light on the **retina** at the back of the eye. Cells in the retina sense brightness, color, and movement. They send signals along the **optic nerve** to the brain.

Cells at the back of the eye sense brightness, color, and movement.

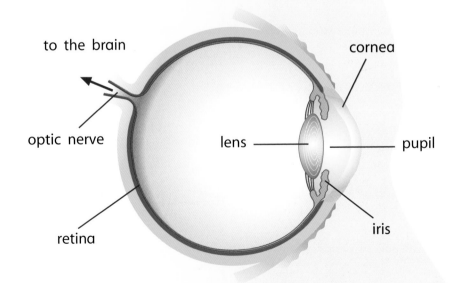

to the brain

cornea

optic nerve

lens

pupil

retina

iris

How seeing helps you

When someone kicks a ball to you, cells in your eyes send messages to your brain. Then your brain sends a message to your feet to tell them to run and kick the ball.

Your eyes help you to kick a ball.

Your sense of sight helps you to understand your surroundings. It lets you see an object's color, size, shape, movement, and distance.

Your eyes help to keep you safe. You use them to look for cars before you cross a road.

You look for cars with your eyes.

Hearing

You hear with your ears. Sounds enter your ears through the **pinna**, which is the part of the ear you can see. The sounds travel along the ear canal to the eardrum. When sounds hit the eardrum, they make it **vibrate**.

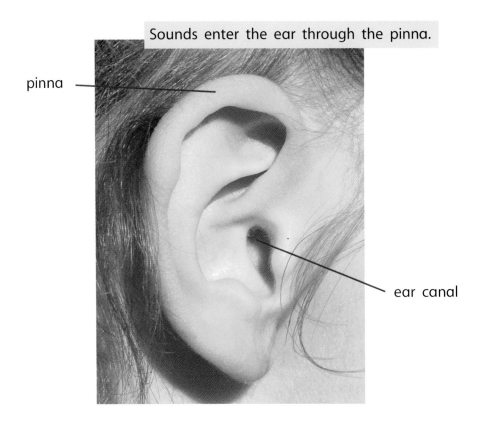

Sounds enter the ear through the pinna.

pinna

ear canal

Vibrations pass from the eardrum along three tiny ear bones to a snail-shaped tube called the **cochlea**. The vibrations make liquid inside the cochlea move. Then hair cells in the cochlea send signals along the auditory nerve to the brain.

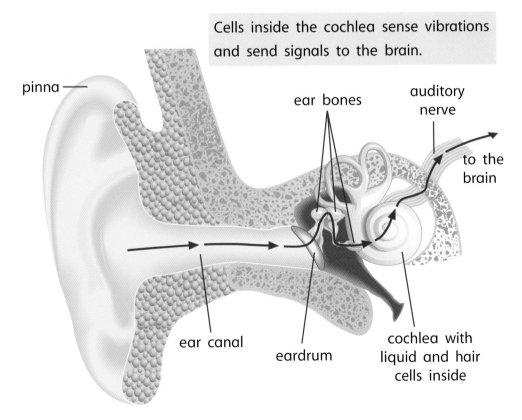

Cells inside the cochlea sense vibrations and send signals to the brain.

pinna

ear bones

auditory nerve

to the brain

ear canal

eardrum

cochlea with liquid and hair cells inside

How hearing helps you

When someone asks you a question, cells in your ears send messages to your brain. Then your brain sends a message to your mouth to tell it to answer the question.

Your ears help you to know when someone is asking you a question.

You listen to music with your ears.

Your sense of hearing helps you to listen to voices, music, and other sounds. Hearing helps you to learn from and talk with other people.

Your ears help to keep you safe. You use them to listen for fire alarms or car horns.

Smelling

You smell with your nose. When you breathe in, air and odors, or smells, travel through your nostrils to your **nasal cavity**. Some of the odors reach two patches of nerve cells at the top of your nasal cavity.

Air and odors enter your nose through your nostrils.

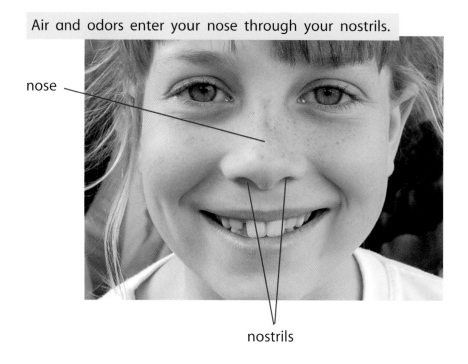

nose

nostrils

The odors **dissolve** in the **mucus** covering the nerve cells. Then the nerve cells send signals to a part of your brain called the **olfactory bulb**. From here messages travel to other parts of your brain.

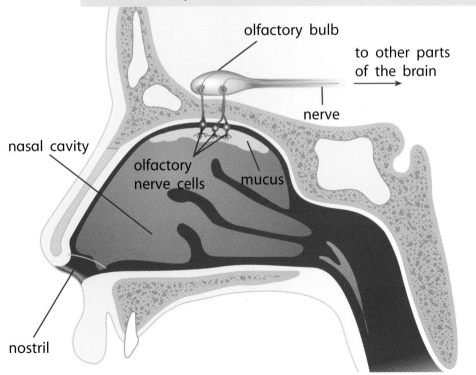

Cells in the nasal cavity sense odors and send messages to the olfactory bulb and other parts of your brain.

olfactory bulb

to other parts of the brain

nerve

nasal cavity

olfactory nerve cells

mucus

nostril

How smelling helps you

When you smell cake, cells in your nose send messages to your brain. Your brain then sends a message to your hand and mouth to tell them to eat the cake.

Your nose helps you to know that cake would taste good.

Your sense of smell helps you to enjoy the flavor of foods and drinks. It lets you enjoy the scent of flowers.

Your nose helps to keep you safe. You use it to smell rotten food, leaking gas, or smoke.

You smell a freshly mown lawn with your nose.

Tasting

You taste with your tongue. The top of your tongue is covered with small bumps called **papillae**. Many papillae have taste buds, which are made up of a group of 50 to 100 taste cells. Taste cells sense sweet, salty, sour, or bitter tastes.

You use your tongue to taste food.

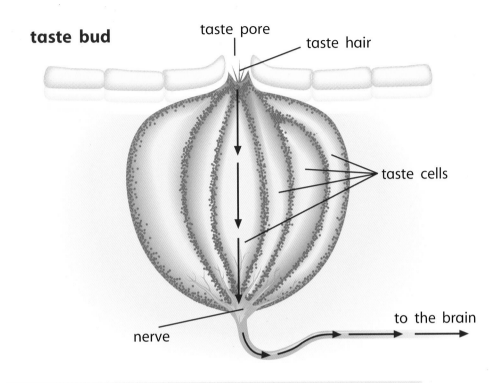

taste bud

taste pore

taste hair

taste cells

nerve

to the brain

Taste cells sense tastes and send messages to your brain.

When you eat, food dissolves in the **saliva** in your mouth. Dissolved food enters a taste bud through an opening called a taste pore. The tiny bits of food touch taste hairs on the taste cells. The taste cells sense tastes and send signals along a nerve to the brain.

How tasting helps you

If you accidentally eat spoiled fruit, cells on your tongue and in your nose send messages to your brain. Then your brain sends a message to your hand and mouth to tell them not to eat the spoiled fruit.

Cells on your tongue help you to know when food is spoiled.

Your sense of taste helps you choose and enjoy food.

Your tongue helps to keep you safe. It warns you when foods such as fruit or meat have gone bad or when milk is sour.

You taste fruit with your tongue.

Touching

You touch and feel things with your skin. Your skin has three layers. The upper layer is the epidermis, and the middle layer is the dermis. The dermis has **touch receptors** and nerve endings to sense how things feel. The bottom, fatty layer protects the body from bumps.

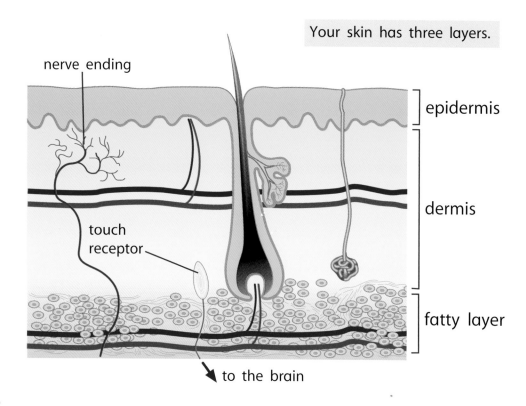

Your skin has three layers.

nerve ending

touch receptor

epidermis

dermis

fatty layer

to the brain

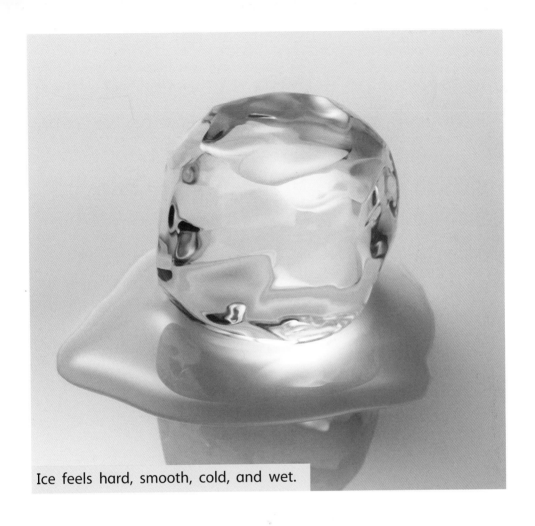
Ice feels hard, smooth, cold, and wet.

When you touch something, touch receptors and nerve endings send signals along nerves to your brain. If you touch ice, touch receptors send messages to your brain to tell you that ice is very cold and hard.

How touching helps you

If you stand on a thistle, nerve endings in the skin on your feet send messages to your brain. Then your brain sends a message to your legs and feet to tell them to move off the thistle.

Nerve endings in your skin help you to know when you stand on a thistle.

Your sense of touch helps you to learn about size, shape, texture, and temperature.

Touching helps to keep you safe. It tells you if something is sharp, such as a knife, or hot, such as a cup of hot chocolate.

Babies learn by touching things with their skin.

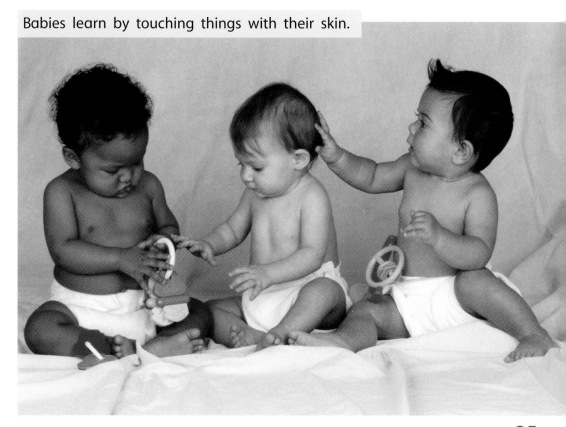

Hunger

Hunger is the feeling you have when you need to eat some food. If you do not eat for several hours, your stomach may feel empty and make a growling sound. These hunger pangs make you want to eat something.

You feel hungry when you need something to eat.

Thirst

Thirst is the feeling you have when you need to drink some water. Every day, your body loses water in wastes, sweat, and the air you breathe out. When your body needs to replace this lost water, you start to feel thirsty.

You feel thirsty when you need a drink.

Balance

Your sense of balance keeps your body steady. When you ride a bike, your inner ears, eyes, skin, muscles, and joints send messages to your brain. Then your brain sends a message to your muscles to tell them how to keep your body balanced.

Your sense of balance helps you to ride a bike.

Pain

Pain is the feeling you have when you are hurt or sick. When you scrape your knee, nerve endings in your skin send messages to your brain. Then your brain tells you how much or how little it hurts and decides what you should do about the pain.

You feel pain when you scrape your knee.

Using All Your Senses

You use one or more of your senses all the time. Your senses collect information and send it to your brain. Your brain uses this information to help you enjoy life and to keep you safe.

Did You Know?
Birds find their way over long distances by using the sun as a compass and by sensing Earth's magnetic field.

Did You Know?
Some snakes can sense the heat given off by birds and mammals.

Did You Know?
Sharks can sense tiny electrical signals sent out by their prey.

Glossary

cochlea	a coiled tube in the ear that is filled with fluid; the cochlea receives sound vibrations from the ear bones.
cornea	the clear outer layer of the eye that covers the iris and pupil
dissolve	to mix something in a liquid so it becomes part of the liquid
focuses	makes a clear picture
lens	a clear part of the eye that bends light rays to focus them on the retina
mucus	a wet, slippery liquid in the nose
nasal cavity	a space behind the nose
olfactory bulb	a part of the brain above the nasal cavity
optic nerve	the nerve that carries messages from cells in the retina to the brain
papillae	the small bumps on the top and sides of the tongue that grip food
pinna	the part of the ear on the outside of the head; the pinna funnels sounds into the ear canal.
pupil	the opening through which light enters the eye; the pupil looks black and changes size.
retina	the inner lining of the back of the eye; the retina contains light-sensitive cells.
saliva	a liquid in the mouth that mixes with food
touch receptors	specialized nerve endings that sense touch, pressure, heat or cold, and send signals along a nerve to the brain
vibrate	to move back and forth quickly

Index

Web Sites

You can go to these web sites to learn more about your senses:

http://www.kidshealth.org/kid/index.html

http://www.howstuffworks.com/question242.htm

http://yucky.kids.discovery.com/noflash/body/pg000008.html